Second Class Activity Book
Contents

GW00602069

 Have you been to a zoo?

1. Read the story. Colour the picture.

A trip to the zoo

David went to the zoo in Dublin. He saw lots of different animals. He liked the monkeys the best. They were playing in the trees and swinging from their tails. David thought they were funny.

Suddenly there was a loud scream. One of the monkeys had escaped. People at the zoo were afraid. A keeper tried to catch the monkey but it jumped high into a tree. The keeper called to the monkey. The monkey would not listen.

'Maybe the monkey will come down for these,' David said. David gave the keeper some bananas.

The keeper showed the bananas to the monkey. The monkey came down and took a banana. Then the keeper picked the monkey up and put him back in with the other monkeys.

'Thank you, young man,' said the keeper to David.

'You saved the day.'

Chimps can live into their 50s.

2. Talk about.

    a.   What would you have done if you saw the monkey escape?

    b.   Talk about how zoos help animals.

3. Complete the answers.

    a.   Where did David go?

    David went _____

    b.   Which animals did he like the best?

    He liked _____

    c.   Why did a person scream?

    A person screamed because _____

    d.   Who tried to catch the monkey?

    The _____

    e.   What did David give to the keeper?

    David gave _____

4. Write the missing words.

> **Remember** Sentences begin with a capital letter.

> one   playing   many   funny   Dublin

    a.   David went to a zoo in _____.

    b.   He saw _____ animals.

    c.   The monkeys were _____ in the trees.

    d.   David thought they were _____.

    e.   _____ of the monkeys escaped.

5. Draw a picture in your copybook to match this sentence.
The monkey jumped high into the tree.

6. Write the sentence.

_____

> Vowels are **a, e, i, o** and **u**.
> All the other letters of the alphabet are called consonants.

7. Say the word. Write the sound at the start of each word.

a e o u

umbrella	___range	___gg	___nt
___ddress	___strich	___mbulance	___lephant

8. Write the missing letter.

a e i o u

___pple	___nder	___ye	___wl	___lien	___nsect

9. Make words.

Add **a**.	Add **e**.	Add **o**.	Add **i**.	Add **u**.
___rt	___nd	___x	___nk	___p
___sh	___ar	___dd	___ll	___s
___xe	___at	___ff	___f	___se
___nd	___xit	___ne	___s	___gly

I am
an adder
not an udder.

10. Read the words.

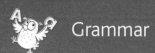

Sentences **begin** with a capital letter and **end** with a **full stop**.

Sample Today the class will work extra hard.

Always try your best.

11. Underline the capital letters and circle the full stops.

a. The sea is full of fish.

b. My dog eats my shoes.

c. Our house is yellow.

d. You are my friend.

e. We are working.

12. Complete the sentences using your own words.

a. The class wants to _____

b. The cat is _____

c. The teacher says _____

d. The boy can _____

e. The girl ran away from _____

13. Write these sentences correctly.

a. my dog can do tricks

_____

b. please give me some cake

_____

c. your father is a rock star

_____

d. the boy ate too many carrots

_____

e. school is the best place to be

_____

Do not forget the full stops.

Word list

catch	lots	playing	their	these

14. Learn the spellings. Now look and say, picture, cover, write, check.

_____   _____

_____   _____

_____

15. Write any words you got wrong.

_____

Can I have **lots** of homework teacher?

16. Write the missing words. Use words from the list.

  a.   The class asked _____
       teacher if they could go home.

  b.   You will not _____ me.

  c.   I want to eat _____ of vegetables.

  d.   The children are _____ in the mud.

  e.   _____ crisps are the best.

17. Find the smaller word in each of these words.

  a.   catch _____   d.   lots _____

  b.   their _____   e.   playing _____

  c.   these _____

Drama

18. Mime a zoo animal. The class must guess what you are.

Write about

19. The pictures tell a story. Write a sentence for each picture. Try using some words from the box.

zoo	Mum	Dad	ticket	animals	lion	roar	fright

_____

_____

_____

_____

_____

20. Find the animals in these mixed up words.

a. onil   _____   e. skena   _____

b. gerti   _____   f. arbe   _____

c. keymon   _____   g. farigfe _____

d. pohip   _____

 Before you read... Have you seen many spiders in your school?

1. Read the fact file. Colour the picture.

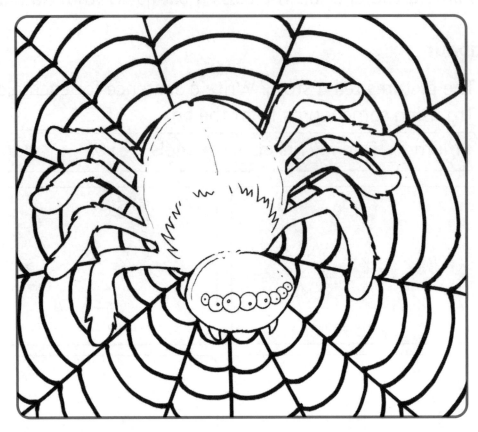

Spiders

Spiders have eight legs.

They can be found almost anywhere in the world.

They are hunters and most of them eat insects but some bigger spiders eat lizards and mice.

Many spiders catch their food in their webs.

These webs are made from silk thread.

Some of these threads are sticky and trap insects.

Some spiders jump on insects to catch them.

Other spiders live in burrows underground and pull insects in through hidden doors.

All spiders have fangs.

Most spiders are not dangerous to people.

Spiders have eight eyes but don't usually see well.

2. Talk about.

   a.   What do you do when you see a spider?

   b.   Talk about how spiders help us.

3. Answer the questions.

   a.   How many legs does a spider have?

      It has _____.

   b.   What are the webs made from?

      Webs are made _____.

   c.   Where in the world can spiders be found?

      Spiders can be found _____.

   d.   How do webs trap insects?

      Webs are _____.

   e.   Name something a bigger spider might eat.

      A bigger spider _____.

4. Write the missing words.

spiders	jump	hunters	not	live

   a.   Spiders are _____.

   b.   Some spiders _____ on insects.

   c.   Some spiders _____ underground.

   d.   All _____ have fangs.

   e.   Most spiders are _____ dangerous.

5. Write the sentences and draw pictures to match.

Spiders catch food in their webs.   Bigger spiders eat lizards and mice.

6. Write the missing letters.

a e i o u

cash	t__sk	w__ng	__gg
st__p	r__n	w__ll	w__t

7. Change the **i** to **e**. Read the new words.

pit _____   tin _____   pig _____   miss _____

sit _____   pin _____   fill _____   pick _____

lit _____   rid _____   bill _____   mind _____

bit _____   big _____   till _____   disk _____

8. Make words.

Add **b.**   Add **c.**   Add **h.**   Add **p.**

__ ut   __ ut   __ ut   __ ut

__ at   __ at   __ at   __ at

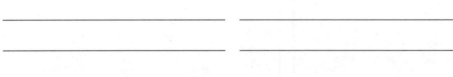

> I wanted ten cookies not tin cookies.

9. Write some more **at** words.

_____   _____

_____   _____

_____   _____

_____   _____

Names of people and pets begin with a capital letter.

> **Sample** The teacher asked **C**olin to dance.

10. Underline the capital letters and circle the full stops.

    a.   I went to Liam's house at the weekend.

    b.   My friends are called Mary, Brigid and Molly.

    c.   The teacher said Josh got his sums right.

    d.   I hope that Kerry is at Bronagh's party.

    e.   The dog called Paws belongs to Thomas.

> **Remember** Sentences begin with a capital letter.

11. Write the sentences, adding capital letters and full stops.

    a.   my mum asked dave to help in the garden

    _____

    b.   brendan and janet are playing in the match

    _____

    c.   my cat jinx loves cold milk

    _____

    d.   eric took his bird tweetie out of the cage

    _____

    e.   we know that derek will win the race

    _____

12. These are your new pets. Give them names.

    a.   rabbit   _____

    b.   cat   _____

    c.   dog   _____

    d.   snake   _____

    e.   dragon   _____

    f.   bird   _____

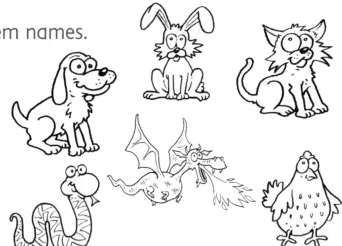

Word list

| found | many | people | pull | eight |

13. Learn the spellings. Now look and say, picture, cover, write, check.

_____   _____

_____   _____

_____

_____

> I have **many** pets.

14. Write any words you got wrong.

_____

15. Write the missing words. Use the word list.

a.   The number between seven and nine is _____.

b.   There were lots of _____ at the festival.

c.   I lost my pen, but then I _____ it.

d.   Do not push the door open, _____ it.

e.   You have had too _____ buns.

16. Write the answers.

a.   Find a smaller word in **many**. _____

b.   Clap the words. Write the number of claps (or syllables).
     many ☐   **people** ☐   **found** ☐   **pull** ☐

c.   Think of a rhyme that will help you to spell **people**.

_____

_____

> A rhyme to remember how to spell **cycle**:
> **C**an **y**ou **c**ook **l**ittle **e**ggs?

Drama

17. Work in a group. Perform this rhyme with actions.

Incey, Wincey Spider,
Climbed up the spout.
Down came the rain and
Washed the spider out.
Out came the sun and
Dried up all the rain.
And Incey Wincey Spider
Climbed up the spout again.

> A fear of spiders is called arachnophobia.
> How many claps in arachnophobia?

Write about

18. Write an acrostic poem using the word spider.

An acrostic poem is written by using each letter of the word **spider**.

S – _____
P – _____
I – _____
D – _____
E – _____
R – _____

Example
S – spinning his web
P – pouncing on his prey
I – in his web waiting for you
D – dare you to pick it up
E – eating flies – yuck
R – really helpful to us

> Use a dictionary to help you.

19. How many words can you make from this word?
Write them in your copybook.

ARACHNAPHOBIA

Before you read... What is your favourite milkshake?

1. Read the recipe. Colour the pictures.

Recipe for banana milkshake

Things you will need:
1 banana
2 scoops of ice-cream
2 cups of milk
1 tablespoon of sugar
2 glasses
1 fork
mixing bowl
1 whisk

1. Wash your hands.
2. Peel the banana and put it into a bowl. Mash it with a fork.
3. Add the sugar and milk.
4. Mix in the ice-cream.
5. Whisk until frothy.
6. Pour into two glasses.
7. Drink and enjoy!

Milk is good for your bones and teeth.

2. Talk about.

   a. Can you make anything to eat or drink by yourself?
   b. Talk about how to be safe in the kitchen.

3. Answer the questions.

   a. What is this recipe for?

      It is for _____.

   b. How many cups of milk do you need?

      You need _____.

   c. What is the first thing you must do?

      You must _____.

   d. What do you use the fork for?

      You _____.

   e. Which sweet thing is added?

      _____.

   > **Remember** Do not forget capital letters and full stops.

4. Write the missing words.

   | frothy | ice-cream | pour | bowl | before |

   a. You will need two scoops of _____.
   b. You can mix it in a mixing _____.
   c. _____ you mash the banana, you must peel it.
   d. Whisk the mixture until it is _____.
   e. _____ it into two glasses.

5. Write the sentences in order.

   Whisk the mixture.   _____

   Drink and enjoy.   _____

   Mash the banana.   _____

   Pour it into two glasses. _____

   Add ice-cream.   _____

   Add sugar and milk.   _____

6. Say the word. Write the sound at the end of the word.

nk   ft   st   ld   nt

| raft | co___ | che___ ___ | pla___ ___ | tru___ ___ |
| so___ ___ | li___ ___ | dri___ ___ | roa___ ___ | pai___ ___ |

7. Circle the correct word.

| belt / bent | wasp / want | mask / mast | tent / test | chimp / child |
| bold / bolt | lamp / land | bunk / bump | dust / dusk | sulk / sunk |

8. Make words.

Add **ink**.
bl___ ___ ___
p___ ___ ___
th___ ___ ___
dr___ ___ ___
w___ ___ ___

Add **ank**.
b___ ___ ___
pl___ ___ ___
t___ ___ ___
th___ ___ ___
Fr___ ___ ___

Add **unk**.
j___ ___ ___
sk___ ___ ___
tr___ ___ ___
ch___ ___ ___
b___ ___ ___

Can you think, wink, drink and blink at the same time?

9. Read the words.

| Remember Sentences begin with a capital |

| Remember Names of people and pets begin with a capital letter. |

Names of places begin with a capital letter.

| Sample Next year we are going to **E**gypt. |

10. Write the missing words.

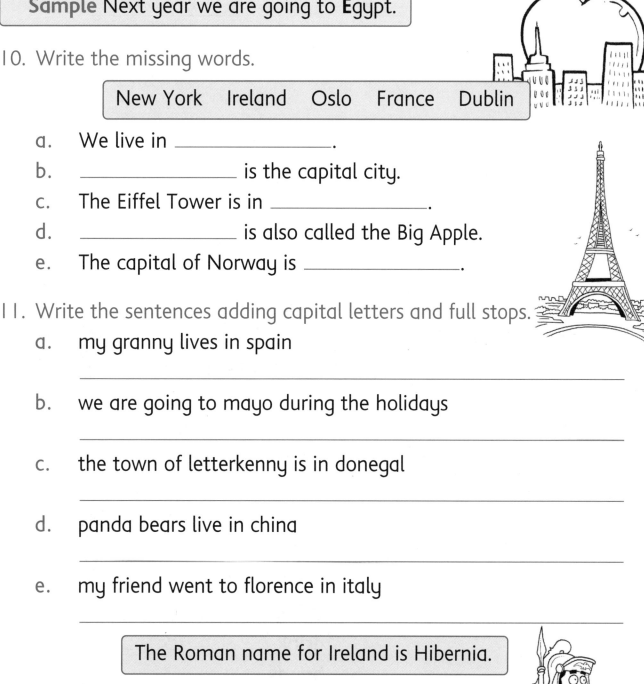

| New York   Ireland   Oslo   France   Dublin |

a.   We live in _____.

b.   _____ is the capital city.

c.   The Eiffel Tower is in _____.

d.   _____ is also called the Big Apple.

e.   The capital of Norway is _____.

11. Write the sentences adding capital letters and full stops.

a.   my granny lives in spain

_____

b.   we are going to mayo during the holidays

_____

c.   the town of letterkenny is in donegal

_____

d.   panda bears live in china

_____

e.   my friend went to florence in italy

_____

| The Roman name for Ireland is Hibernia. |

12. Complete the sentences.

a.   I live in the town of _____.

b.   It is in County _____.

Word list

| until   wash   things   drink   hands   enjoy |

13. Learn the spellings. Now look and say, picture, cover, write, check.

_____   _____

_____   _____

_____   _____

14. Write any words you got wrong.

_____

15. Write the missing words. Use the word list.

> If you're happy and you know it, clap your **hands**.

| **Remember** Sentences begin with a capital letter. |

   a.   I love to _____ cold milk.

   b.   I hope you _____ your day.

   c.   _____ your hands before dinner.

   d.   Get your school _____ ready.

   e.   Clap your _____ for the teacher.

   f.   I will not talk _____ my work is done.

16. Write the answers.

   a.   Find smaller words in **enjoy** _____

                        wash _____

                        things _____

                        drink _____

                        hands _____

   b.   Clap the words in the word list.

   c.   How many words have one clap (or syllable)? ☐

   d.   How many words have two claps (or syllables)? ☐

Drama

17. Work with a friend. Follow the recipe and make banana milkshakes.

> A dairy cow gives about 16 litres of milk a day.

Write about

18. Write a simple recipe for something you know how to make. It can even be a cup of tea or a sandwich.

RECIPE FOR _____

Things you will need: _____

_____

_____

Things to do: _____

_____

_____

_____

_____

19. Match up the beginnings and endings of these words to find five dairy products.

Example: | yog | + | hurt | = | yoghurt |

che	ice-	eam
mi	tter	ese
bu	cr	ik
cream		

_____

_____

_____

_____

_____

20. Which dairy products do you like?

_____

Have you ever had a fever?

1. Read the picture story. Colour the pictures.

Sick in bed

On Tuesday morning Lisa woke up. She did not feel well. Her head was sore and she felt weak.

Her Mum came into the room.

Mum put her hand on Lisa's forehead. It felt hot.

Later that day Lisa and her Mum went to the doctor.

Lisa took the medicine. It tasted horrible.

Three days later Lisa was feeling much better. It was time to go back to school.

Never take medicine unless an adult gives it to you.

2. Talk about.

   a.   What does it feel like to have a fever?

   b.   Talk about keeping and taking medicine safely.

3. Answer the questions.

   a.   On which day did Lisa feel sick?

   _____

   b.   Who came into Lisa's room?

   _____

   c.   How did her forehead feel?

   _____

   d.   Who did Mum ring?

   _____

   e.   What did the doctor give to Lisa?

   _____

4. Write the missing words.

| doctor | said | head | horrible | Lisa |

   a.   Lisa's _____ was sore.

   b.   Her Mum _____ she would be late for school.

   c.   Mum told _____ to rest.

   d.   The _____ said Lisa had a fever.

   e.   The medicine tasted _____ .

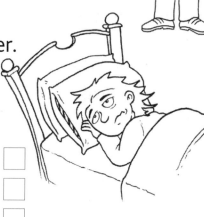

5. Put the sentences in order.

   a.   Three days later, Lisa felt better. ☐

   b.   The doctor said she should stay in bed. ☐

   c.   Lisa and her Mum went to the doctor. ☐

   d.   Lisa took the medicine. ☐

   e.   Lisa did not feel well. ☐

6. Write the missing letter.

| a | e | i | o | u |

| apron | ___tter | dr___m | sw___m |
| ___lf | cl___ck | ch___ps | cr___st |

7. Circle the correct word.

| splash / thrash | band / bank | went / west | string / spring |
| desk / dent | lamp / lump | sand / send | tap / trap |

8. Make words.

Add **amp**.

st___ ___ ___
d___ ___ ___
c___ ___ ___
r___ ___ ___
tr___ ___ ___

Add **ump**.

b___ ___ ___
j___ ___ ___
st___ ___ ___
p___ ___ ___
l___ ___ ___

I need a cab not a crab.

9. Read the new words you just made.

Days of the week, months of the year and special days begin with a capital letter.

> **Sample** This year **S**aint **P**atrick's **D**ay falls on **S**aturday the 17th **M**arch.

10. Underline the capital letters. Circle the full stops.

a. This Christmas we will see Santa.

b. James and Marie are coming home on Tuesday.

c. They celebrate Diwali in India.

d. For Saint Valentine's Day, Mark will give Sarah a rose.

e. There is a beautiful castle in Kilkenny.

On November the 3rd, they have Sandwich Day in America.

11. Write the answers.

a. What day will it be in two days time? _____

b. On what day of the week is your birthday this year?

_____

c. Name one special day in December. _____

d. Which is your favourite month of the year? _____

e. Which month is the start of spring? _____

12. Write the sentences adding capital letters and full stops.

a. lee and i are going to dublin in may

_____

b. i will take part in the saint patrick's day parade

_____

c. this hallowe'en luke will be a vampire

_____

d. my cousin niamh lives in limerick

_____

Word list

did	few	school	days	feeling	much

13. Learn the spellings. Now look and say, picture, cover, write, check.

_____   _____

_____   _____

_____   _____

14. Write any words you got wrong.

_____

> **School days** are the best days.

15. Write the missing words. Use the word list.

  a. Lorraine has a _____ sums left to do.

  b. Gerry _____ make his bed.

  c. The class is _____ tired.

  d. We spend most of the day at _____.

  e. The weekend is two _____.

  f. I like milkshakes very _____.

16. Write the answers.

  a. Find a smaller word in **feeling**. _____

  b. Clap the words. Write the number of claps (or syllables).

    school ☐   **did** ☐   **feeling** ☐

  c. Look at the words from the word list. Sort them by their first letter.

d	f	s	m

Drama

17. Work with a friend. Act a scene about a doctor and a sick patient.

Write about

18. Write a note from a parent to the teacher explaining why you were not able to go to school.

Dear _____

_____

_____

_____

_____

_____

From _____

19. Complete the wordsearch.

w	e	r	t	d	s	l	e	e	p	y	s
i	o	m	e	d	i	c	i	n	e	a	n
s	d	o	f	g	c	r	n	u	r	s	e
g	h	h	j	l	k	z	j	x	c	b	e
r	c	o	u	g	h	f	e	v	e	r	z
r	e	s	t	b	n	m	c	l	t	u	e
w	e	p	i	l	l	s	t	r	p	t	y
u	i	i	o	n	p	a	i	f	s	d	f
j	k	t	o	l	z	d	o	c	t	o	r
v	b	a	n	m	r	t	n	u	y	w	e
n	f	l	m	n	b	v	c	x	s	d	f

doctor
medicine
rest
fever
sick
pills
cough
sleep
nurse
hospital
injection
sneeze

 Before you read...

Have you ever seen a camel?

1. Read the text. Colour the pictures.

The camel

The camel lives in the desert.

It is very hot in the desert.

Some camels have one hump but others have two.

The camel keeps fat in its hump.

This can be turned into food and water.

The camel has two joined toes.

This is so it does not sink into the sand.

It also has two sets of eyelashes to protect its eyes from the sun and the sand.

The camel can close its nostrils to block out sand.

A camel can go a long time without food or water.

When there is water, it can drink two hundred litres at one time.

It eats grass and grain.

The camel is called the ship of the desert.

The camel has very bad breath.

2. Talk about.

Why do you think the camel is called the ship of the desert?

3. Answer the questions.

a. Where does the camel live?

_____

b. What does the camel keep in its hump?

_____

c. Why does it have two sets of eyelashes?

_____

d. Why does it have joined toes?

_____

e. What does the camel eat?

_____

f. What is the camel called?

_____

4. Write the missing words.

| food | water | hot | drink | close | hump |

a. It is very _____ in the desert.
b. Some camels have one _____, others have two.
c. The camel can _____ its nostrils.
d. It can go a long time without _____ or water.
e. It can _____ 200 litres of water in one go.
f. The fat in its hump can be turned into food and _____.

5. Draw a camel in your copybook. Use these words as labels.

| hump | eyelashes | nostrils | joined | toes | tail | mouth |

When we read **ph** we use a **f** sound.

| **Sample ph**ot**ograph** |

I asked for a plate of chips not ships.

6. Add **ph** to these words. Draw the pictures.

ele____ ____ant	tele____ ____one	al____ ____abet	geogra____ ____y

7. Say the word. Write the missing sounds.

| th   ch   sh   wh   ph |

phone	____eese	____ale	____umb	____urch
____oto	____irty	____eep	____eel	____adow

8. Sort the words by their first letter sounds.

| shark   whisk   then   cherry   what   chicken   shoe   thing |

ch	sh	th	wh

The letter **i** on its own is a word for **me** and takes a capital letter. Titles like Mr. or Doctor also begin with a capital letter.

> **Sample I** think **I** would like to meet **M**r. **S**impson.

9. Underline the capital letters and circle the full stops.

   a. My teacher is called Miss. Neat.
   b. Jim and I are going to visit Mr. Donkey.
   c. We all think Dr. Spock is cool.
   d. I asked Mrs. Muffin to bake a cake.
   e. The class greeted Fr. Murray.

10. Write the missing words. Make up some titles and names.

   a. Our teacher is called _____.
   b. The doctor I go to is _____.
   c. The principal of the school is called _____.
   d. Another teacher in our school is _____.

> **Remember** Capital letters and full stops.

11. Write the sentences correctly.

   a. we think miss jones gives us too much homework _____

   _____

   b. katie and i go to football on wednesdays _____

   _____

   c. i have to see doctor green about my sore foot _____

   _____

   d. we saw prince william in london _____

   _____

Word list

very	does	eyes	long	hot	close	without

12. Learn the spellings. Now look and say, picture, cover, write, check.

_____   _____

_____   _____

_____   _____

_____

13. Write any words you got wrong.

_____

14. Write the missing words. Use the word list.

a.   _____ your eyes and go to sleep (but not now).

b.   I am _____ happy I got a puppy.

c.   My brother cannot go _____ his teddy.

d.   Brad _____ drink milk every day.

e.   It is _____ in the desert.

f.   She ties up her _____ hair.

g.   Open your _____ and look at me.

15. Write the answers.

a.   Which word from the list ends with **yes**? _____

b.   Which word starts with **do**? _____

c.   Break **without** into two smaller words.

_____   _____

I will not get square **eyes**.

d.   Clap the words in the list.
     Which words have two claps (or syllables)?

_____

_____

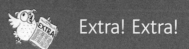
Drama

16. Work in a group. Choose an animal. Describe yourself to the group. The group must guess which animal you are.

Write about

17. Choose an animal. Find out five facts about it. Write them here.

_____

_____

_____

_____

_____

_____

> The camel has a huge stomach.

18. Name the animal.

| panda | cheetah | monkey | zebra | giraffe | snake | elephant |

a. I am spotty. I am the fastest animal. _____

b. I am the tallest animal on earth. _____

c. I have big ears and a trunk. _____

d. I have black and white stripes. _____

e. I have black and white fur. _____

f. I do not have legs or feet. _____

g. I swing from branches in trees. _____

 Before you read... Name a restaurant you have been to.

1. Read the menu. Colour the menu.

Children's Corner
Fast food made good

Menu

Roast chicken	€3.00
Pasta	€3.00
Fish sticks	€2.00
Toasted sandwiches	€3.00
Omelette	€3.00
Baked potato	€2.00
Green salad	€2.00
Vegetables	€2.00

Desserts

Ice-cream and chocolate sauce	€3.00
Fruit salad	€3.00

Sit and enjoy.

2. Talk about.

   a. What else could be on the menu?

   b. Talk about good manners when you are eating in a restaurant.

3. Answer the questions.

   a. What is the name of the restaurant?

   _____

   b. How many items are there on the menu?

   _____

   c. What kind of chicken can you order?

   _____

   d. What is served with the ice-cream?

   _____

   e. Which is more expensive, the omelette or fish sticks?

   _____

   f. Name a healthy item on the menu.

   _____

4. Answer **yes** or **no**.

   a. You can order chips with your meal. _____

   b. There is fruit for dessert. _____

   c. Vegetables cost €2.00 _____

   d. You can order pasta. _____

   e. Egg is not on the menu. _____

   f. Bread is an item on the menu. _____

5. In your copybook work out the total cost of this bill.

> ### Children's Corner
> 049-019527986
>
> Order: 1 pasta, 2 green salads, 2 sandwiches,
> 4 fruit salads, 1 ice-cream

The magic **e** at the end of a word makes the other vowel say its name.

> **Sample** gave

6. Add the **magic e** to these words. Read the new words.

cap___	man___	spin___
rod ___	pin___	cub___
rob___	hat___	tub___

7. Write the missing letters. Add the **magic e** at the end.

sm___l___	g___t___	k___t___	b___n___
t___n___	n___s___	b___k___	c___s___

8. Write the missing **magic e** words.

> gate   these   fine   note   late   June

a. I am feeling _____ today.

b. Leave a _____ to say where you are.

c. Do not be _____ for school.

d. The month before July is _____.

e. The teacher wants _____ children to stay in at break.

f. Close the _____.

I hope that you like this page.

34

Questions end with a **question mark**.

> **Sample:** What is in the box?

9. Complete the sentences with a question mark
    or a full stop. Write out the sentences.

    a. Claire loves apples

        _____

    b. Where are my shoes

        _____

    c. When can we go outside

        _____

    d. I want to swim in the sea

        _____

    e. Who is the teacher talking to

        _____

10. Write the missing word and question mark.

    | why | where | when | which | who |

    a. _____ did you put my apple

    b. _____ do you want to sit next to

    c. _____ child has the best manners

    d. _____ is the teacher angry today

    e. _____ can we go home

Are you having fun?

11. Write a simple question for the answer.
    Remember to add the question mark.

    a. Answer: green

        Question: _____

    b. Answer: two

        Question: _____

    c. Answer: school

        Question: _____

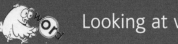
Word list

| salad | fruit | pasta | green | children | sit | fast |

12. Learn the spellings. Now look and say, picture, cover, write, check.

_____   _____

_____   _____

_____   _____

_____

A fruit is your friend.

13. Write any words you got wrong.

_____

14. Write the missing words. Use the word list.

    a.   A _____ can have tomatoes, lettuce and cucumber.

    b.   The _____ were not afraid of the dragon.

    c.   I do not like the colour _____.

    d.   Bananas, grapes and peaches are types of _____.

    e.   You need to boil _____ before you eat it.

    f.   _____ down at your desk.

    g.   The hare can run very _____.

15. Write the answers.

    a.   Which words have **as** in them? _____ _____

    b.   Write the **st** words from the list. _____

    c.   Which word starts with **child**? _____

    d.   Which words ends with **it**? _____ _____

Drama

16. Work with a friend. One person is the waiter and the other is a customer. The waiter must take the order and repeat it to see if he or she gets it right. Take turns.

Write about

17. Write a menu you would like to see.

18. Which items do not belong on the menu?

    a.   Circle them.

    b.   What should they be?

    _____

    _____

    _____

    _____

    _____

    _____

    _____

    _____

    _____

Crazy kid café	
Omelette with hat	€4.00
Chicken and ice	€4.00
Sausages and mush	€4.00
Curry and mice	€5.00
Fish bricks and chins	€2.00
Vegetable soap	€2.00
Pork shops and rice	€3.00
Chocolate rake	€2.00
Apple tie and cream	€2.00

Before you read...

Have you ever lost something?

1. Read the poem. Colour the picture.

Trouser hunt

I can't seem to find my trousers,
I've looked in every place.
I've looked in my entire room,
They've vanished without trace.

I looked in all the wardrobes,
And behind the bedroom door.
I went through all the clothes,
That were lying on the floor.

I checked through all the dresser drawers,
And under the duvet too,
Behind the blind, and under the bed,
And even in the loo!

I've turned everything upside down,
Where on earth could they be?
Now I see them! There they are!
My trousers are on me!

2. Talk about.

    Do you think the poet's room was tidy?

3. Answer the questions.

    a.   What did the poet lose?

    _____

    b.   In which room was he looking?

    _____

    c.   What was lying on the floor?

    _____

    d.   What does the poet have on his bed?

    _____

    e.   What does he have on the windows?

    _____

    f.   Where did he find what he was looking for?

    _____

4. Draw four places the poet looked.

5. Put the sentences in order.

    He looked:

    a.   Behind the blind   ☐

    b.   In the wardrobes   ☐

    c.   In the loo   ☐

    d.   Under the bed   ☐

    e.   Behind the bedroom door ☐

    f.   In the dresser drawers ☐

6. Add the **magic e** to these words. Read the new words.

cod___   pip___   rid___

can___   tap ___   fin___

kit___   pop___   not___

7. Write the missing letters. Add the **magic e** at the end.

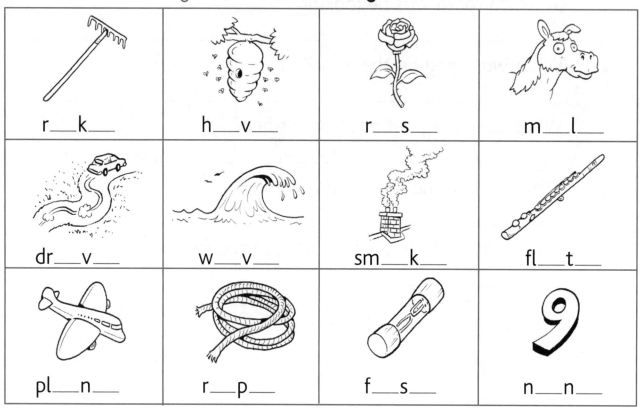

r___k___	h___v___	r___s___	m___l___
dr___v___	w___v___	sm___k___	fl___t___
pl___n___	r___p___	f___s___	n___n___

8. Write the missing **magic e** words.

| slide | size | cave | rude | broke |

a. The _____ is full of bats.

b. My shoe _____ is three.

c. Who _____ the window?

d. Jeff is going down the _____.

e. You should not be _____.

Your Mum did not write this note.

9. Underline the capital letters. Circle the full stops.
    Put squares around the question marks.
    a.   My Dad's name is Danny.
    b.   Mr. and Mrs. Noon live in Sligo.
    c.   Amy and Pat are in Spain until Thursday.
    d.   What do you wish for this Christmas?
    e.   Why is Doctor Green moving to England in April?

10. Write the sentences adding capital letters, full stops
    and question marks.
    a.   this saturday brendan is buying easter eggs

    _____

    b.   who told miss smith that eoin was bold

    _____

    c.   i wish i lived in a city like dublin or london

    _____

    d.   my cat is called socks and my dog is prince pooch

    _____

    e.   when is peter taking us to cork

    _____

    | **Remember** Capital letters, full stops and question marks. |

11. Write your own sentences using these words. Do not forget the
    punctuation marks.
    a.   Wexford   _____
    b.   Why   _____
    c.   I   _____
    d.   Mr.   _____
    e.   January   _____

Word list

| can't | find | every | behind | could | looked | door | even |

12. Learn the spellings. Now look and say, picture, cover, write, check.

_____   _____

_____   _____

_____   _____

_____   _____

> I do exercise **every** day.

13. Write any words you got wrong.

_____

14. Write the missing words. Use the word list.
   a.   Lock the _____ when you are alone.
   b.   Kathy _____ for her teddy but could not find it.
   c.   _____ if it rains we still have to run laps.
   d.   I wish I _____ fly like a bird.
   e.   Did you hide _____ the tree?
   f.   The teacher cannot _____ her red pen.
   g.   I wish I could come to school _____ day.
   h.   Jackie _____ go to town as she is busy.

15. Write the answers.
   a.   Find smaller words in   **find**   _____
                                every   _____
                                behind   _____
   b.   Which four words from the word list end with **d**?

   _____ _____ _____ _____

   c.   Do they sound the same at the end?_____
   d.   Write two words from the list that begin with **e**.

   _____ _____

   e.   Which word ends with **or**? _____

Drama

16. Work in a group. You are looking for something. The group must guess what you are looking for. Give them clues.

Write about

17. Write a poem about looking for something.
    Try to rhyme lines 2 and 4, 6 and 8, 9 and 10.

    I cannot find my _____,

    I've looked just everywhere,

    I looked _____,

    And I looked _____.

    I looked in _____,

    And I looked _____,

    I looked in _____,

    And I looked _____.

    Oh where on earth is my _____?

    _____

18. Follow the instructions.

   a. Colour the boy's shirt blue.
   b. Make orange spots on his trousers.
   c. Colour his hair yellow.
   d. Colour one shoe green and the other yellow.
   e. Draw a book in his hand.

What birds have you seen before?

1. Read the text. Colour the picture.

The cuckoo

Every spring the cuckoo returns to Ireland.

It comes from warmer countries in Africa where it has spent the winter.

The cuckoo is quite a lazy bird.

She does not build her own nest.

She waits for other birds to lay their eggs.

Then when the mother bird is away, she lays one of her eggs in the nest.
Then she gets rid of one of the other eggs, and flies away.

When the mother bird comes back, she does not notice the different egg.

She sits on all the eggs to keep them warm and safe.

The cuckoo egg hatches first.

The baby cuckoo is pink and has no feathers.

It pushes the other eggs out of the nest.

Now it can get all the food the parents bring.

What a cheeky bird.

2. Talk about.
   a. Why is the cuckoo called a cheeky bird?
   b. How can we help birds in winter?

3. Answer the questions.
   a. When does the cuckoo return to Ireland?

   _____

   b. Where does it spend the winter?

   _____

   c. Where does the cuckoo lay her eggs?

   _____

   d. What colour is the baby cuckoo?

   _____

   e. What does the baby cuckoo do to the other eggs?

   _____

   f. Why does the baby do this?

   _____

4. Write the missing words.

build	lazy	safe	cuckoo	no	one

   a. The cuckoo is a _____ bird.
   b. She does not _____ her own nest.
   c. She lays _____ of her eggs in another bird's nest.
   d. The bird sits on the eggs to keep them warm and _____.
   e. The _____ egg hatches first.
   f. The baby cuckoo has _____ feathers.

5. Write a sentence about what you think of the cuckoo.

   _____

All these can make an **a** sound as in **pay**.

eigh	ay	ai	ei	ea	ey

6. Write the missing letters.

eigh	ay	ai	ea

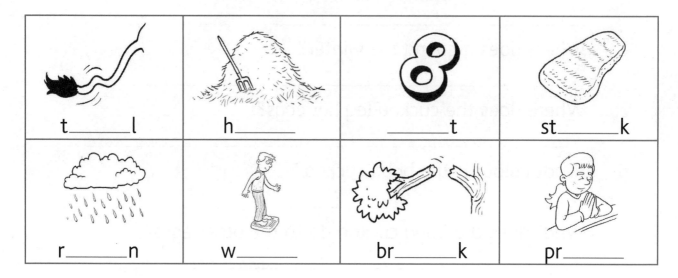

t_____l   h_____   _____t   st_____k

r_____n   w_____   br_____k   pr_____

7. Circle the correct word.

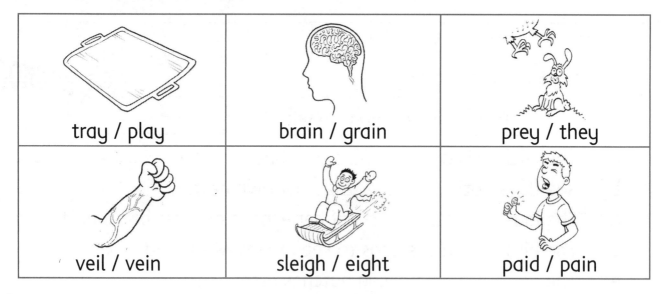

tray / play   brain / grain   prey / they

veil / vein   sleigh / eight   paid / pain

8. Make words. Read the new words.
   Add **ai**.

   j__ __l   p__ __nt
   m__ __n   st__ __n
   ch__ __n   tr__ __n

They have **eight steaks** every day.

Nouns are naming words. They can be names, places or things.

> **Sample** Molly, Wexford, dog, teacher, desk, sun

9. Circle the nouns.
   a. The hedgehog was in our garden.
   b. David and Conor went to the movies in Dublin.
   c. The book is in the library.
   d. Cian had three bananas in his lunchbox.
   e. Gedus comes from Poland.

Do your **work** well for the teacher.

10. Write the missing nouns.

> mouse   game   room   spoon   tree

   a. Please tidy your _____.
   b. Switch your _____ off now.
   c. Did you feed the _____?
   d. Do not climb that _____.
   e. Use a _____ to eat soup.

11. Choose the correct noun. Write the sentence.
   a. The hen is laying (eggs, cars, birds).

   _____

   b. My homework is on the (door, lake, table).

   _____

   c. The cat chased the (flower, rat, cake).

   _____

   d. On Mondays I go to (the moon, school, the fridge).

   _____

   e. I sleep on a (window, bed, cooker).

   _____

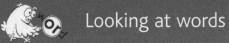

Word list

quite   own   spring   mother   bring   winter   first   warm

12. Learn the spellings. Now look and say, picture, cover, write, check.

_____   _____

_____   _____

_____   _____

_____   _____

> The teacher forgot to **bring** our books to school.

13. Write any words you got wrong.

_____

14. Write the missing words. Use the word list.

    a.   I hope I come _____ in the race.

    b.   In _____, blossoms appear on the trees.

    c.   Jessie will _____ a cake to school.

    d.   I wish I had my _____ room.

    e.   Niamh did her spellings _____ well.

    f.   Charlie's _____ is very kind.

    g.   Some animals sleep for the _____.

    h.   Wear your hat to keep your head _____.

15. Write the answers.

    a.   Find smaller words in

          quite _____   **spring** _____

          mother _____   **bring** _____

          winter _____   **warm** _____

    b.   Which two words are names of seasons?

          _____   _____

    c.   Which word begins with a vowel? _____

Drama

16. Pretend to be a cuckoo. Act out the cuckoo's story.

Write about

17. Find pictures of a cuckoo. Draw a cuckoo and colour it correctly. Write five sentences about the cuckoo in your copybook.

The cuckoo likes to eat insects.

18. Write the birds in the grid below.

							f	
				r				
			c					
w						l		
w			o					

wren	eagle
osprey	chat
robin	thrush
jay	lark
wagtail	finch
crow	owl

Is a fox a clever or a silly animal?

1. Read the story. Colour the picture.

The fox and the crow

One evening a crow was flying home to his nest.

When he passed over a farmyard, he saw a big piece of cheese on the ground.

He flew down and picked it up.

Then the crow flew to a branch to sit and eat it.

A hungry fox was out looking for food.

He saw the crow with the piece of cheese in his beak.

He wanted the cheese so he made a plan.

'Good evening, Mr. Crow. How are you?' the fox shouted.

The crow said nothing.

'You look very well this evening,' said the fox.

Still the crow said nothing.

'I heard that you have a beautiful singing voice. I wonder if you could sing for me,' said the fox.

The crow was pleased when he heard this.

He opened his beak to sing.

'Caw! Caw! Caw!'

The cheese fell out of his mouth.

The fox grabbed the cheese and ran away.

The crow knew that the fox had made a fool of him.

2. Talk about.

What should the crow have done?

3. Answer the questions.

a. What did the crow see on the ground?

_____

b. Where did he go to eat it?

_____

c. Who saw the crow?

_____

d. What did he ask the crow to do?

_____

e. How did the cheese fall out of the crow's mouth?

_____

f. Who ate the cheese?

_____

4. Write the missing words.

a. The crow was _____ home to his nest.

b. He saw a _____ piece of cheese.

c. The fox was _____ for food.

d. The fox had a _____.

e. The crow opened his _____ to sing.

f. The crow knew the fox had made a _____ of him.

5. Put the sentences in order.

a. The cheese fell out of his beak. ☐

b. The fox grabbed the cheese. ☐

c. The fox had a plan. ☐

d. The crow saw a piece of cheese. ☐

e. The crow sang for the fox. ☐

f. The crow sat in a tree to eat it. ☐

All these can make an **e** sound as in **see**.

ee	ey	ea	ie

6. Write the missing letters.

ee	ey	ea

b__ __	mon__ __	l__ __f	s__ __
turk__ __	f__ __t	chimn__ __	sl__ __p

7. Circle the correct word.

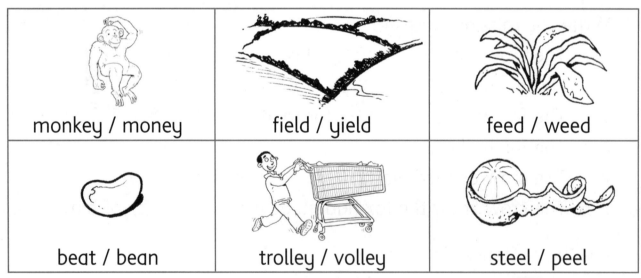

monkey / money	field / yield	feed / weed
beat / bean	trolley / volley	steel / peel

8. Make words. Read the new words.

Add **ee**.

b__ __n
h__ __l

Add **ea**.

b__ __n
h__ __l

> Feed yourself on wheat and honey.

A verb is an action word.

> **Sample** He **walks** to school. The school **is** close by.

9. Underline the verbs.

   a.   Mum drives us to school.
   b.   The kitten plays with the wool.
   c.   We write all day in school.
   d.   The teacher talks a lot.
   e.   The class is very good.

10. Write the missing verbs. Use the words from the box.

> were   fell   swim   read   bark

   a.   She _____ off her chair.
   b.   You should _____ a book every day.
   c.   The dog will _____ at the birds.
   d.   They _____ in the playground.
   e.   May I _____ in the lake?

11. Choose the correct verb for each sentence.

   a.   The elephant _____ through the jungle.
        (skips, crashes, swings)
   b.   The tiger _____ at me.
        (squeaks, chirps, roars)
   c.   The boy _____ milk every day.
        (eats, drinks, walks)
   d.   This school _____ boys and girls.
        (has, was, is)
   e.   The green frog _____ at night.
        (giggles, purrs, croaks)

Word list

branch	sing	over	wanted	nothing
heard	his	knew	passed	

12. Learn the spellings. Now look and say, picture, cover, write, check.

_____   _____

_____   _____

_____   _____

_____   _____

_____

> I **heard** the bell for **home** time.

13. Write any words you got wrong.

_____

14. Write the missing words. Use the word list.

a. I _____ tea but I got coffee.

b. My Dad likes to _____ in the shower.

c. The cow jumped _____ the moon.

d. Enda knew _____ spellings were good.

e. My sister _____ her driving test.

f. The owl sat on the _____ of the tree.

g. Paul _____ a funny noise.

h. I _____ it was going to rain today.

i. There is _____ to do at home.

15. Write the answers.

a. Which word from the list starts with **hear**?

_____

b. Which word has **in** in it? _____

c. Break **nothing** into two smaller words. _____

d. Find smaller words in   **wanted**   _____

                        his   _____

                        knew   _____

                        passed   _____

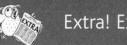
Crows live alone or in pairs.

Drama

16. Work with a friend. Act out the story of the fox and the crow.

Write about

17. Write a sentence for each picture in your copybook.
    The pictures tell a story.

18. Circle the odd one out.

    a. milk, yoghurt, cheese, apples, butter
    b. tree, flower, weed, rose, sand
    c. robin, cat, crow, thrush, blackbird
    d. kennel, nest, chair, stable, burrow
    e. big, small, huge, massive, large
    f. eat, look, desk, fly, sing
    g. badger, deer, hedgehog, fox, cow
    h. evening, clock, morning, afternoon, night
    i. six, nine, one, pen, three
    j. plum, banana, plan, pig, pull

 Before you read...

Have you ever written a letter to someone?

1. Read the letter.

Dear Shane,

I hope you are well.

My family and I went camping in the country.

We stayed in a tent.

It was not a good holiday.

We were there for five days and it rained every day.

Everything got wet — our clothes, our food and us.

The tent leaked and we had to sweep the water out.

The beach was nearby but it was too cold to go there.

We tried to have a barbecue a few times, but my Dad could not get it right. We ate mostly soggy cereal every day.

We had planned to go on many walks.

Instead we sat inside the tent reading books and being bored.

I am so happy to be home where it is warm and dry!

It would be great if you could spend a weekend at my house.

Your friend,

Gerry

2. Talk about.

   Why did Gerry have a bad holiday?
   What activities can we do if the weather is wet?

3. Answer the questions.

   a.   Who wrote the letter?

   _____

   b.   Where did the family go?

   _____

   c.   How many days did it rain?

   _____

   d.   Why did they not go to the beach?

   _____

   e.   What activity did they do in the tent?

   _____

   f.   What did they mostly eat?

   _____

> **Remember** Sentences start with a capital letter and end with a full stop.

4. Write the missing words.

   a.   The letter was written to _____.

   b.   The _____ leaked.

   c.   Dad could not get the _____ right.

   d.   They had _____ to go on walks.

   e.   Gerry was happy to be _____.

   f.   Shane is Gerry's _____.

5. Write what you think was the worst part of his holiday.

   I think _____

   _____

6. Write the missing letters.

| ch | sh | wh | th | ph |

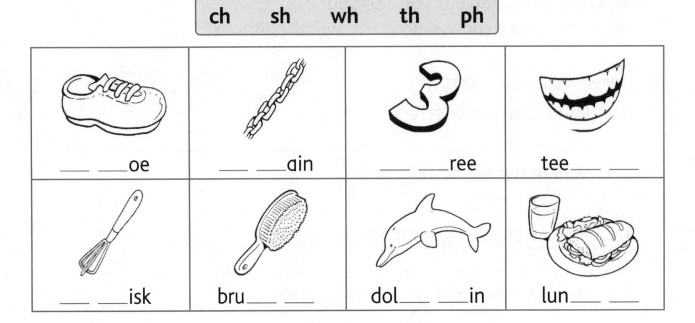

____ ____oe   ____ ____ain   ____ ____ree   tee____ ____

____ ____isk   bru____ ____   dol____ ____in   lun____ ____

7. Add the **magic e** to these words. Read the new words.

plan____   slid____   cut____   win____   rip____   hid____

pal____   mat____   pip____   fir____   pan____   grim____

8. Circle the correct word.

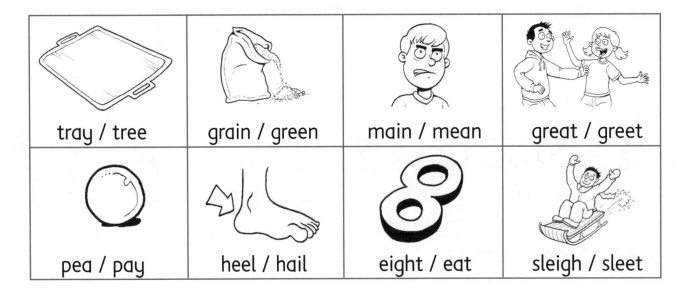

| tray / tree | grain / green | main / mean | great / greet |

| pea / pay | heel / hail | eight / eat | sleigh / sleet |

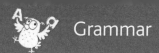
Adjectives are describing words. They tell you more about the noun.

> **Sample** The **grumpy** dragon bit the **bold** child.

9. Circle the adjectives.

> You are a **kind**, **lovely** and **sweet** child.

a. The yellow bird ate a slimy worm.
b. The good girl got a great prize.
c. The hot children jumped into the cool pool.
d. The brown bread was eaten by a hungry mouse.
e. My smelly socks are in my messy room.

10. Complete the sentences.

> soft   dirty   wooden   steep   cold
> chocolate   sweet   old   silly   gentle

a. The _____ car could not get up the _____ hill.
b. The _____ lambs ate the _____ grass.
c. My _____ pillow is on the _____ chair.
d. The _____ biscuit fell on the _____ floor.
e. My _____ brother threw _____ water at me.

11. Write two adjectives for each noun.

dog

tree

cake

shirt

monster

_____   _____   _____   _____   _____

_____   _____   _____   _____   _____

> Use interesting words.

Word list

family	five	nearby	friend	because
cold	holiday	right	tent	

12. Learn the spellings. Now look and say, picture, cover, write, check.

_____   _____

_____   _____

_____   _____

_____

> It is **cold** today.

13. Write any words you got wrong.

_____

> A way to remember how to spell **because** is:
> **B**etty **e**ats **c**arrots **a**nd **u**ncle **s**ells **e**ggs.

14. Write the missing words. Use the word list.

a. In winter my toes get _____.

b. Fifteen take away _____ is ten.

c. My _____ and I do everything together.

d. There is a bank _____.

e. There are two children in our _____ .

f. We have to get our sums _____.

g. The class is staying in _____ it is snowing.

15. In your copybook write two sentences with **holiday** and **tent**.

16. Write the answers.

Find smaller words in **family** _____

nearby _____

friend _____

Drama

17. Work with a group. Perform a scene from a family holiday.

Write about

18. Write a short letter to your friend. Tell him or her about a day out that you have had.

Dear _____

_____

_____

_____

_____

_____

_____

_____

From _____

19. Who are these people? Read their envelopes for the clues.

This person lives in a place opposite to sweet. The street is named after the girl who lost her sheep.

Name: _____

> Dr. Cheep
> Apartment 2A
> Weak Street

This person does not live in a house. The road name sounds the same as the word for seven days.

Name: _____

> Mr. White
> Munchy Meats
> Wells

This person is a butcher. He or she lives in a town that rhymes with **yells**.

Name: _____

> Fr. Duffy
> 7 Bo Peep Street
> Sour Town

Before you read...

Do you think a lion could be friends with a rabbit?

1. Read the story. Colour the picture.

The rabbit and the lion

Lion: Good day, Mr. Rabbit, and how do you do?

Rabbit: Don't come any closer, I do not trust you.

Lion: Now, now, Mr. R, there's no need to fear.

Rabbit: I'll scream so loudly if you come near!

Lion: Relax, I'm not hungry, in fact, I just ate.

Rabbit: I bet you would like to see me on your plate.

Lion: Hah! You're just a starter, just a small scrap!

Rabbit: Yes, well I'm off now before I get trapped.

Lion: Ah, that is a pity, stay and chat with me.

Rabbit: Goodbye, Mr. Lion, please let me go free.

Lion: Hey, sure, Mr. Bunny, but come visit my den,

I look forward to eating you, I mean, meeting you again!

2. Talk about.

What did the lion really want? Talk about staying safe.

3. Write the missing words.

a. The rabbit met a _____.

b. He did not _____ the lion.

c. The lion said he was not _____.

d. The rabbit was afraid he would get _____.

e. The lion _____ the rabbit to stay.

f. He invited the _____ to his den.

g. The lion wanted to _____ the rabbit.

4. Answer **yes** or **no**.

a. The lion greeted the rabbit. _____

b. The lion ate the rabbit. _____

c. The rabbit said he would scream. _____

d. The rabbit was afraid of the lion. _____

e. The lion chased the rabbit. _____

f. The rabbit asked to go free. _____

g. The lion wanted to be friends with the rabbit. _____

5. Write some speech for the lion and the rabbit. Use your own words.

These can make an **i** sound as in **ice**.

igh	ie

6. Write the missing letters.

igh	ie

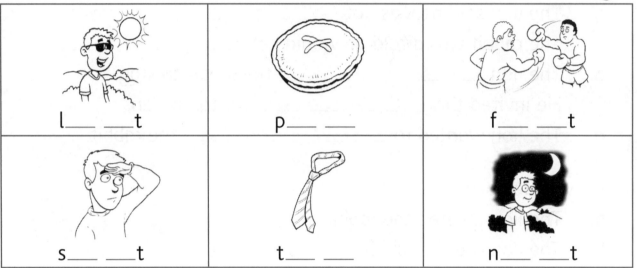

l___ ___t   p___ ___   f___ ___t

s___ ___t   t___ ___   n___ ___t

7. Circle the correct words.

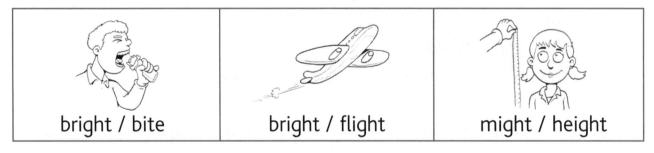

| bright / bite | bright / flight | might / height |

8. Use these words to write sentences of your own. Underline the **i** sounds.

right	tight	bright	might

_____

_____

_____

_____

Plurals mean more than one. Sometimes we add **s** to make words more than one.

> **Sample** pen – pens

If a word ends in **s**, **x**, **sh** or **ch**, we add **es** to make more than one.

> **Sample** fox – foxes

9. Add **s** to these words to make them plural.

a. bed___   f. book___

b. eye___   g. toy___

c. flower___   h. car___

d. sock___   i. window___

e. chair___   j. door___

10. Add **es** to these words to make them plural.

a. match___   f. watch___

b. kiss___   g. box___

c. brush___   h. dish___

d. class___   i. ash___

e. ditch___   j. switch___

11. Circle the plural words.

a. The witches were making potions to turn boys into frogs.

b. My wishes are to get games, a phone and books.

c. Mum got dresses for my sisters.

d. Kate had peaches and plums in her lunchbox.

e. Boys and girls must sit on the benches.

Word list

near	small	off	before	please
trust	visit	don't	any	mean

12. Learn the spellings. Now look and say, picture, cover, write, check.

_____   _____

_____   _____

_____   _____

_____   _____

_____   _____

> I am **sure** it was here **before**.

13. Write any words you got wrong.

_____

14. Write the missing words. Use the word list.

a. My cousin from France is coming to _____.

b. _____ you go to bed, brush your teeth.

c. Get your elbows _____ the table.

d. You can _____ me with your money.

e. You used to be _____ but now you are big.

f. Always say _____ when you want something.

g. _____ play with matches.

h. The school is _____ to a church.

15. In your copybook, write sentences using the words **any** and **mean**.

16. Write the answers.

a. Which word from the list has **ear** in it? _____

b. Which word from the list ends with **all**? _____

c. Which words ends with **it**? _____

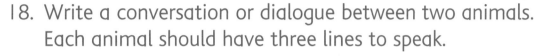

Drama

17. Work with a friend. Read the story of the rabbit and the lion. Take turns to be the rabbit and lion.

Write about

18. Write a conversation or dialogue between two animals. Each animal should have three lines to speak.

Animal	What they are saying
_____	_____
_____	_____
_____	_____
_____	_____
_____	_____
_____	_____

> A lion's home is called a den.

19. Complete the creature word ladder. Each creature must begin with the last letter of the word before.

owl	rhino
elephant	ape
duck	tiger
lion	koala
natterjack toad	

rabbit

 Before you read...

Do you know a rescue story?

1. Read the story. Colour the picture.

Rescue

One day Sinéad and Brian were in the park.

They were kicking the ball to each other.

Sinéad was kicking the ball too high.

Suddenly she kicked it right into a tree.

'Oh no,' said Brian. 'That is my new ball. I will try and get it.'

Brian climbed up the tree until he got to the ball.

'I have it,' he shouted.

But when he looked down, he became afraid.

'Are you coming down?' asked Sinéad.

'I can't,' said Brian. 'I am too high up.'

'Wait there, Brian. I will get some help,' shouted Sinéad.

Sinéad ran home to get her Dad.

Sinéad's Dad brought a long ladder.

He climbed up the ladder and helped Brian to get down.

'You should not have climbed so high,' said Sinéad's Dad. 'You could have fallen and hurt yourself.'

'Oh no!' said Brian.

'What is the matter now?' asked Sinéad.

'I left the ball up in the tree!' said Brian.

2. Talk about.

   How can Brian get the ball out of the tree?

3. Answer the questions.

   a.   Where were Brian and Sinéad playing?

   _____

   b.   What were they playing with?

   _____

   c.   Who kicked it into a tree?

   _____

   d.   What did Brian do then?

   _____

   e.   Why did Brian need help?

   _____

   f.   Who came to help?

   _____

   g.   Did Brian get the ball?

   _____

4. Write the missing words.

   a.   Sinéad was kicking the ball too _____.

   b.   It was Brian's _____ ball.

   c.   Brian _____ up the tree.

   d.   When he looked down, he became_____.

   e.   Sinéad ran to get _____ Dad.

   f.   Sinéad's Dad brought a _____ ladder.

   g.   Brian left the ball in the _____.

5. What would you have done to get to the ball?

   _____

   _____

These can make an **o** sound as in **bone**.

ow	oe	oa

6. Write the missing letters.

ow	oe	oa

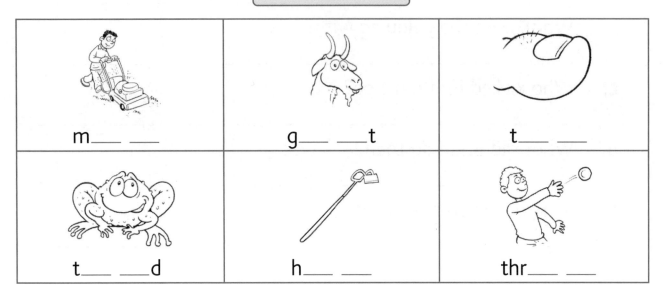

m___ ___   g___ ___t   t___ ___

t___ ___d   h___ ___   thr___ ___

7. Circle the correct word.

snow / flow   doe / poem   soap / boat

8. Make words. Read the new words.

Add **ow**.	Add **oe**.	Add **oa**.
sl___ ___	J___ ___	f___ ___m
gr___ ___	f___ ___	s___ ___p
gl___ ___	p___ ___t	l___ ___f

She should be kissing a toad.

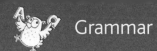

9. Turn these words into plural words.

> **Remember** If a word ends in **s**, **x**, **ch**, or **sh**, add **es**.

latch   _____   bush   _____

crash   _____   school   _____

mug   _____   pitch   _____

glass   _____   desk   _____

stitch   _____   boss   _____

10. Underline the letters that should be capitals. Write the sentences correctly in your copybook.

    a.   mr. and mrs. duffy are going on a trip to south africa

    b.   on wednesdays i have coaching with phil

    c.   my cat jessie loves to play with my dog jack

    d.   peter is going to play tricks on the teacher on april fools day

11. Sort the nouns, verbs and adjectives. Write them in the correct box.

> bear   clever   sings   bold   child   is
> teacher   big   plays   silly   house   eats

Nouns	Verbs	Adjectives

12. Write four sentences using words from this table.

_____

_____

_____

_____

Word list

each	high	try	became	should
left	park	kicking	coming	asked

13. Learn the spellings. Now look and say, picture, cover, write, check.

_____   _____

_____   _____

_____   _____

_____   _____

_____   _____

Left!
Right!

14. Write any words you got wrong.

_____

15. Write the missing words. Use the word list.

   a.   Shane is _____ the ball into the nets.

   b.   You _____ eat vegetables every day.

   c.   I _____ talk now as I have work to do.

   d.   At night the ghost _____ afraid.

   e.   You must _____ to have good manners.

   f.   The inspector is _____ to visit our school.

   g.   _____ child in the class will get a prize.

16. In your copybook write sentences using the words **high**, **left** and **asked**.

17. a.   Write two words that rhyme. _____

    b.   Do they have the same spelling pattern? _____

18. Write the number of claps (or syllables).

left [ ]   kicking [ ]   coming [ ]   asked [ ]

Drama

19. Work with a group. Act out the scene in the *Rescue* story.

Write about

20. Complete this rescue story.

One day Rachel and Benny were playing in the lake. It was a hot day and they were splashing in the water. Suddenly they heard someone shouting for help. They looked out at the lake.

There they saw _____

_____

_____

_____

_____

_____

_____

_____

21. Crack the code. Write the message.

A	B	C	D	E	F	G	H	I	J	K	L	M
■	▲	▶	▼	◀	●	□	O	⊙	♥	◆	✖	⚡

N	O	P	Q	R	S	T	U	V	W	X	Y	Z
◣	⬒	⊕	✚	✪	⮺	✳	⊞	⊞	☺	⚑	⅄	✿

■✖☺■⅄⮺ ▲◀ ⮺■●◀ ☺O◀◣ ⅄⬒⊞ ⊕✖■⅄

_____ _____ _____ _____ _____ _____

Write your own message. Can your friend work it out?

_____

 Name some creatures that live in the sea.

1. Read the text. Colour the picture.

The octopus

The octopus lives in the sea.

It has eight arms called tentacles.

If it loses an arm, another one will grow.

The octopus has a large head and a very soft body.

The octopus will keep safe by hiding in rocks.

It can squirt ink at animals that are chasing it.

Sometimes an octopus can change its colour.

The octopus eats lobsters, crabs and other shellfish.

It will grab its food with its tentacles.

It will then poison it.

The octopus has a beak-like mouth.

This is hard and sharp so it can break open the shells of its food.

A baby octopus is smaller than a pea, but it has to take care of itself soon after birth.

The octopus is a very clever creature.

The pupil of the octopus's eye is a rectangle shape.

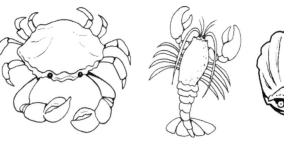

2. Talk about.

Talk about different sea creatures.

3. Answer the questions.

a. How many arms does the octopus have?

_____

b. What are its arms called?

_____

c. Where does the octopus hide?

_____

d. What can it squirt at animals?

_____

e. Name one thing an octopus eats.

_____

f. What kind of mouth does an octopus have?

_____

g. How big is a baby octopus?

_____

4. Write the missing words.

a. The octopus lives in the _____.

b. If it loses an arm _____ one will grow.

c. It has a _____ body.

d. Sometimes an octopus can change its _____.

e. It _____ its food with its tentacles.

f. Its _____ is hard and sharp.

g. The baby octopus takes care of _____.

5. Write a sentence about an octopus.

_____

These can make a **u** sound as in **tube**.

> | ew | ue | eu |

6. Write the missing letters.

> | ew | ue |

st____ ____	tiss____ ____	cr____ ____	stat____ ____

7. Write your own sentences using these words. Underline the **u** sounds.

> flew   chew   rescue   Europe   argue

_____

_____

_____

_____

_____

8. Make words. Read the new words.

Add **ew**.   Add **ue**.

f___ ___   bl___ ___

n___ ___   cl___ ___

vi___ ___   gl___ ___

gr___ ___   tr___ ___

ch___ ___   f___ ___l

Chew your stew.

9. Write a silly sentence using some **u** sound words from this page.

_____

A preposition makes links between words.

> **Sample** I am going **with** my teacher **to** the play.

> **Examples** at, on, in, under, from, by, below, to, above, onto, into, between, along, out, before

10. Circle the prepositions.

    a.   Do not run around the classroom.

    b.   There is a park near my house.

    c.   I want that spider off my bed.

    d.   I am at school sitting under my desk.

    e.   Ben jumped over the wall and into a puddle.

> Before you go out to play, thank the teacher for the work.

11. Write the correct preposition.

> **up   before   out   to   above**

    a.   Tidy your room _____ you go and play.

    b.   The plane is flying _____ the clouds.

    c.   May I go _____ the quiz?

    d.   Pick the baby _____ and pat her.

    e.   We are going _____ to dinner.

12. Write sentences using these prepositions. Underline the prepositions.

> **on   in   with   by   from**

_____

_____

_____

_____

_____

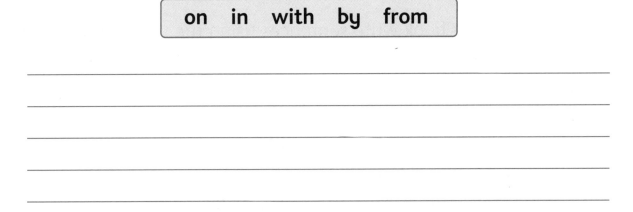

Word list

> sea   called   another   soft   grow
> sometimes   its   hard   break   soon   sharp

13. Learn the spellings. Now look and say, picture, cover, write, check.

_____   _____

_____   _____

_____   _____

_____   _____

_____

Sometimes I sit and think and sometimes I just sit.

14. Write any words you got wrong.

_____

15. Write the missing words. Use the word list.

    a.   The dog was chasing _____ own tail.

    b.   I would like _____ piece of cake.

    c.   Mum _____ me to come in for dinner.

    d.   Whales live in the _____.

    e.   _____ I get tired of working.

    f.   Be careful, the knife is _____.

    g.   I _____ tomatoes and carrots in my garden.

16. In your copybook write sentences using the words **hard**, **soft**, **break** and **soon**.

17. Write the answers.

    a.   Which words starts with **an**? _____

    b.   Find a smaller word in **soft**. _____

    c.   Break **sometimes** into two smaller words.

         _____   _____

Drama

18. Work with a group. Mime a sea creature.
    The group must guess which creature you are.

Write about

19. Find out about another sea creature. Write five facts about it.

_____

_____

_____

_____

_____

20. Follow the instructions to create an undersea picture.

    a. Colour the octopus a grey colour.

    b. Draw sand at the bottom.

    c. Draw a small yellow fish under the octopus.

    d. Draw a bigger red fish on top of the octopus.

    e. Draw two shells on the sand, one in each corner.

    f. Draw two bubbles coming from the red fish's mouth.

    g. Draw a rock in the sand next to the shell on the left.

    h. Draw a shell in one of the tentacles.

    i. Draw a baby octopus in the top right corner.

    j. Draw seaweed in the sand next to the shell on the right.

What time do you go to sleep?

1. Read the poem. Colour the pictures.

Is everyone in bed now?

'Not I,' said the baker,
'I'm making new bread.
I stay up all hours
To keep you well fed.'

'Not I,' said the captain
Who trawls the deep sea.
'Your chips would be lonely
If it wasn't for me.'

'Not I,' said the cleaner
Whose truck spins a brush.
'Night streets are empty.
I miss all the rush.'

'Not I,' said the printer
With ink on the drum.
'If I slept, there'd be
No *Times*, *Beano* or *Sun*.'

'Not I,' said the doctor
Who's always on call.
'I'm ready for you
Should you slip, crash or fall.'

'Not I,' said the midwife
Who sees children born.
'A baby won't hold on
And wait until dawn.'

'Not I,' said the beggar
Who slumps by a door.
'There's no bed for someone
Who's homeless and poor.'

Steve Turner

> *The Times* and *The Sun* are newspapers.

2. Talk about.

Talk about the people in the poem.

3. Answer the questions.

a. What is the baker doing?

_____

b. What is *The Sun*?

_____

c. Who is on call if you hurt yourself?

_____

d. What is the captain doing?

_____

e. Why are the streets cleaned at night?

_____

f. What does a midwife do?

_____

g. What is a beggar?

_____

4. Write the missing words.

a. The _____ makes newspapers.

b. The baker stays up all _____.

c. The _____ is always on call.

d. The captain is out at _____.

e. The cleaning truck has a _____ on it.

f. The _____ helps babies.

g. The beggar is _____.

5. What time do you go to bed? _____

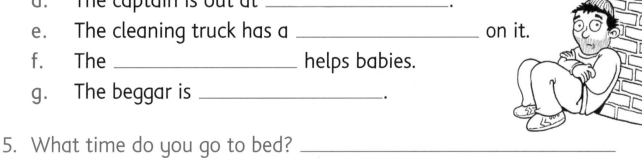

When words end in **le** the **e** is always silent.

> **Sample** candle, fiddle, rubble, sparkle, pickle, tingle

I am in a little muddle.

6. Write the missing word endings.

ble	dle	tle	kle

an**kle**	bub_____	han_____	bot_____
ta_____	rat_____	buc_____	sad_____

7. Write the correct word.

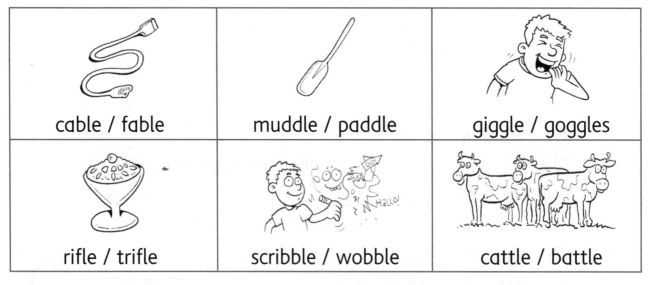

cable / fable	muddle / paddle	giggle / goggles
rifle / trifle	scribble / wobble	cattle / battle

8. Make words. Read the new words.

Add **ble**.	Add **dle**.	Add **gle**.	Add **fle**.
mum__ __ __	mid__ __ __	jun__ __ __	raf__ __ __
nib__ __ __	pud__ __ __	sin__ __ __	shuf__ __ __

9. Circle and write the two smaller words in these words.
   a. matchstick _____ _____
   b. waterfall _____ _____
   c. somewhere _____ _____
   d. birthday _____ _____
   e. afternoon _____ _____
   f. blackbird _____ _____
   g. sunflower _____ _____

10. These compound words are mixed up. Write them correctly.

   Sample shipfish goldwreck – goldfish shipwreck

   a. handcloth / tablebag _____
   b. blacklight / moonboard _____
   c. classman / snowroom _____
   d. sunpaste / toothflower _____
   e. seabow / rainside _____

11. Write the sentences adding capital letters, full stops and question marks.
   a. when is mr smith taking us for art

   _____

   b. i can't wait to give tracey her gift at christmas

   _____

   c. helen and i are leaving for derry on sunday

   _____

   d. miss honey is moving to new zealand in august

   _____

Word list

fed	slept	doctor	crash	whose
empty	lonely	baby	poor	ready	brush

12. Learn the spellings. Now look and say, picture, cover, write, check.

_____ _____

_____ _____

_____ _____

_____ _____

_____

> Oops, I think I slept in.

13. Write any words you got wrong.

_____

14. Write the missing words. Use the word list.

a. The car and the tractor had a _____.

b. The _____ wanted his bottle.

c. Are you _____ for the holidays?

d. The _____ gave me some pills.

e. I _____ in a tent last night.

f. _____ trousers are those?

g. I have no money and my wallet is _____.

15. In your copybook write sentences using the words **brush**, **night** and **poor**.

16. Write the answers.

a. Which word starts with **who**? _____

b. Which word ends with **ash**? _____

c. Find smaller words in **ready** and **poor**.

_____ _____

Drama

17. Work with a group. Mime someone doing
their job. The group must guess which job you do.

Write about

18. Choose a job and write a poem about it in your copybook.
You do not have to write full sentences.

The job: _____

Where you work: _____

What you wear: _____

Things you may use: _____

What you do: _____

A name: _____

> **Example**
> Nurse,
> In a hospital,
> In a white uniform,
> Pills and injections,
> Caring for the sick,
> Nurse Maggie

19. Match the people to their jobs. Write their jobs below what
they do.

I train you to kick the ball.	I make your sick cat better.	I write books for you to read.	I star in movies. I am famous.

_____ _____ _____ _____

I can fly you all over the world.	I sell meat and chicken.	I cook you a delicious meal.	I care for your teeth.

_____ _____ _____ _____

I fix your car when it breaks down.	I give you work to do.

chef coach actor teacher

pilot vet dentist author

mechanic butcher

_____ _____

 Before you read...

Teasing someone is never right. How does it make the person feel?

1. Read the story. Colour the picture.

The ugly duckling

Father Duck and Mother Duck looked at their nine little ducklings.
They had just been born but there was still one big egg left.
Suddenly there was a tapping sound.
Soon a duckling came out of the shell.
But he was not small, yellow and fluffy like the others.
He was big, grey and ugly.
When the ducklings walked around the farm,
all the animals laughed at the big duckling.
No-one played with him.
He was very sad and he left the farmyard.
Now the ugly duckling was all alone.
Winter came and he was cold and hungry.
All the lakes and ponds were frozen.
The poor duckling almost died.
Then a kind farmer found him.
He picked him up and took him home.
He put the duckling by the fire and gave him some food.
When spring came, the duck went out to swim on the pond.
He saw three beautiful white birds with long necks swimming there.
'They will tease me and say I am ugly,' thought the duck.

Then the duck saw his own reflection in the water.
He was not ugly and he was not a duck.
He was a milk-white swan with a lovely long neck.
The other swans said, 'Come with us to the prince's palace.
It is a good life there.'
Away the four swans flew to the palace.
There the ugly duckling lived happily with plenty of food and
lots of friends.

2. Talk about.

Talk about teasing and bullying.

3. Answer the questions.

a. How many eggs were there altogether?

_____

b. What did the last duckling look like?

_____

c. What did the farm animals do?

_____

d. What did the ugly duckling do?

_____

e. Who found him?

_____

f. When did he go out onto the pond?

_____

g. What had he turned into?

_____

4. Write the missing words.

a. The other ducklings were _____ and fluffy.

b. No-one _____ with the ugly duckling.

c. He was cold in the _____.

d. The farmer gave the _____ some food.

e. The duckling saw three _____ birds.

f. The _____ said he must go with them.

g. The four swans _____ to the palace.

5. What should you do if someone is bullying you?

_____

_____

6. Write the correct word sounds.

ow   oa

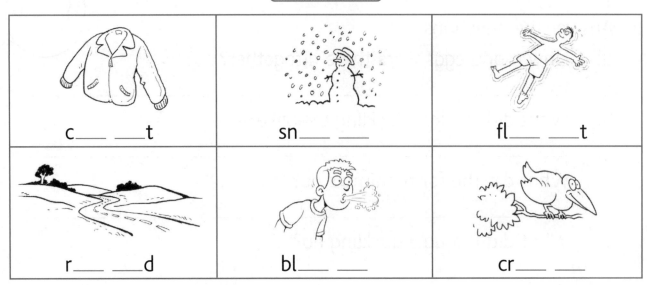

c___ ___t   sn___ ___   fl___ ___t

r___ ___d   bl___ ___   cr___ ___

7. Circle the correct word.

low / row   sight / light   pie / tie

toe / foe   few / new   glue / true

8. Make words. Read the new words.

I will giggle if you tickle me.

Add **ble**.   Add **dle**.   Add **gle**.

nib___ ___ ___   cra___ ___ ___   jun___ ___ ___

peb___ ___ ___   la___ ___ ___   trian___ ___ ___

When we write in the **past tense**, sometimes we add **ed** to the verb.

Sample	fetch – fetched

If a word already ends in **e** we drop the **e** and add **ed**.

Sample	save – saved

9. Write these words in the past tense:

talk - _____   dance - _____

race - _____   bath - _____

dive - _____   bake - _____

jump - _____   cook - _____

love - _____   chase - _____

10. Write the sentences in the past tense by changing the verbs in brackets.

a. Jackie (pour) the tea for the parents.

_____

b. I (gobble) up the sweet buns.

_____

c. The group (hike) in the mountains.

_____

d. The class (laugh) at the funny film.

_____

e. Enda (like) doing Maths in the morning.

_____

11. Write a sentence about what you did yesterday.
Yesterday I _____

_____

Word list

still	yellow	around	almost	gave	small
farm	swim	lovely	lived	alone	little

12. Learn the spellings. Now look and say, picture, cover, write, check.

_____   _____

_____   _____

_____   _____

_____   _____

_____   _____

_____   _____

Is it safe to **swim** here?

13. Write any words you got wrong.

_____

14. Write the missing words. Use the word list.

   a.   Mum _____ me pasta for lunch.

   b.   Pigs, cows and sheep live on a _____.

   c.   The opposite of large is _____.

   d.   Jen likes to _____ in the pool.

   e.   Keep _____ while you hold that spider.

   f.   Run _____ the field every day.

   g.   I do not like to be home _____.

15. In your copybook write sentences using the words **almost**, **small**, **lovely**, **lived** and **yellow**.

16. Write the answers.

   a.   Which word from the list ends with **most**? _____

   b.   Which word from the list ends with **all**? _____

   c.   Which word starts with **love**? _____

Drama

17. Work with a group. Act out the story of *The ugly duckling*.

Write about

18. What do you think the characters are saying? Write it in the speech bubbles.

19. Follow the instructions to work out the message.

Take **g** away from **dog**. _____

Add a **t** to the end of **no**. _____

Unscramble the word **aughl**. l_____

Take **ch** away from **chat**. _____

Add **ot** to the front of **hers**. _____

Take **b** and **n** away from **born**. _____

Change **n** to **r** in **hunt**. _____

Add **ir** to the end of **the**. _____

Add **ings** to **feel**. _____

20. Write the message.

_____

_____

If you could make a wish, what would you wish for?

1. Read the story. Colour the picture.

The magic bottle

One day Mark was walking along the beach gathering shells.

Then he saw a bottle.

He picked up the bottle and pulled out the cork.

Suddenly a genie appeared.

'Aaaaaaahhhhhh,' screamed Mark.

'Do not be afraid,' said the genie. 'This is your lucky day. I will grant you three wishes.'

'That is wonderful,' said Mark.

Mark thought and thought.

'I think my first wish is to have the biggest bicycle,' he said. 'My second wish will be to have a giant ice-cream. My third wish is to have no homework for a whole week.'

'Your wishes will be granted,' said the genie. 'Now I am just going to pop myself back in the bottle. Please put the cork back on and throw me back into the sea.'

Mark did as the genie asked.

Suddenly a large bicycle appeared.

Mark climbed onto the bicycle.

He could not reach the pedals.

Then, a huge ice-cream appeared in his hand.

It was delicious but too big to hold.

It was melting faster than Mark could eat it.

Mark pushed the bicycle home.

Maybe his brother could ride it.

He threw the rest of the ice-cream away because he was just too full.

The next day at school, Mark waited to see if his third wish would come true.

'Now, children,' said the teacher, 'You will have no homework for a week.'

Mark was very happy.

Then the teacher said, 'You will have no homework because you will have to work on the history project.'

'Oh no!' said Mark. 'I wish I had made better wishes!'

2. Talk about.

What should Mark have wished for?

3. Answer the questions.

a. Where was Mark walking?

_____

b. What was he doing?

_____

c. What did he find?

_____

d. What popped out of it?

_____

e. How many wishes did Mark get?

_____

f. What was his second wish?

_____

g. What work did the teacher give the class?

_____

4. Write the missing words.

a. Mark threw the _____ back into the sea.

b. He could not _____ the pedals of the bike.

c. The ice-cream was too big to _____.

d. He would give the bike to his _____.

e. He threw the _____ away.

f. Mark had no _____ as he had to do a project.

g. Mark was _____ with his wishes.

5. Write two wishes you have.

_____

_____

6. Write the missing letters.

st	sk	sp

de____ ____	cri____ ____	____ ____ar
____ ____ull	we____ ____	____ ____ade

7. Add the **magic e** to these words. Write a sentence using each new word.

　　a.　shin　_____

　　b.　sit　_____

　　c.　mad　_____

　　d.　gap　_____

　　e.　bit　_____

Use a dictionary if you need to.

8. Make words. Read the new words.

Add **ind.**	Add **ost.**	Add **int.**
k__ __ __	l__ __ __	pr__ __ __
m__ __ __	m__ __ __	spr__ __ __
h__ __ __	fr__ __ __	m__ __ __

9. Write the missing preposition.

| from | at | into | to | under |

a. Put the broccoli _____ the pot.
b. There is an old pizza _____ your bed.
c. My Mum is _____ bingo tonight.
d. Ben got purple trousers _____ his aunt.
e. I am going _____ bed now.

10. Write the sentences correctly.
    a. on the 26th december it is st. stephen's day

    _____

    b. kevin and i are doing a project on france

    _____

    c. why does bill want to go to galway

    _____

    d. the class does singing with miss smith on mondays

    _____

11. Write the sentences in the past tense by changing the verbs in brackets.
    a. The boy (grumble) about all the work.

    _____

    b. The children (clean) their bedrooms.

    _____

    c. Jack (tumble) down the hill.

    _____

    d. My friend has (move) to Italy.

    _____

    e. He (hope) that it was Friday.

    _____

Carroll Education Limited
34A Lavery Avenue
Park West Industrial Estate
Nangor Road
Dublin 12

http://www.carrolleducation.ie

Copyright © Janna Tiearney 2007
Commissioning Editor: Helen Dowling
Managing Editor: Maggie Greaney
Publishing Consultant: Gay Judge
Designer: Derry Dillon
Print Origination: Design Image
Illustrator: Derry Dillon

First published April 2007. Reprinted 2008. This reprint May 2009.

ISBN: 978-1-84450-090-1